The Archaeology

Peter Herring

Cornwall County Council
Cornwall Archaeological Unit

The Archaeology of Kit Hill

Kit Hill viewed from Stoke Climsland graveyard. Many of those who spent their working lives on the hill are buried here.

Kit Hill, the dominant landscape feature in East Cornwall, visible from Morwenstow to Maker and towering over Callington and Kelly Bray, is an archaeological treasure store. This booklet presents an historical background for the unenclosed upper slopes, now a Country Park, managed by the Coast and Countryside Unit of the Planning Directorate of Cornwall County Council. It is also a guide to the principal sites. It is intended to be of value and interest both to visitors and to the large numbers of local people who regularly explore this well-loved place. It is based on a detailed survey by the Cornwall Archaeological Unit undertaken in the late 1980s. A comprehensive report is also available from CAU, Kennall Building, Old County Hall, Station Road, Truro.

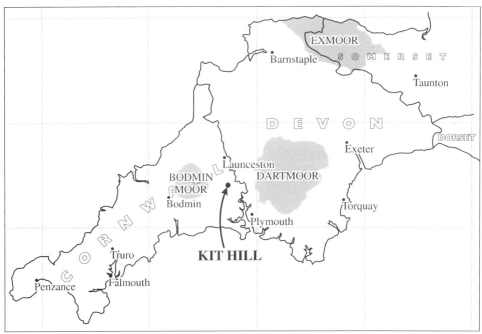

Location of Kit Hill.

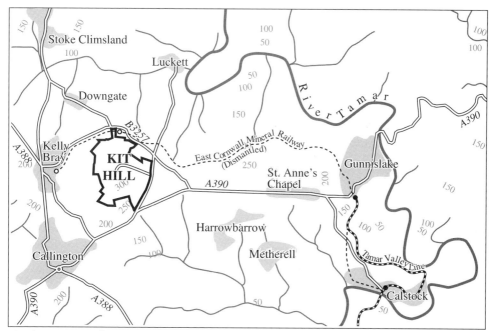

Road access to Kit Hill

The Country Park

Kit Hill Country Park was established in 1985 when Cornwall County Council accepted on behalf of the people of Cornwall, the gift of the Hill's unenclosed land from Prince Charles, Duke of Cornwall, to mark the birth in 1982 of Prince William. The Duke expressed his desire that the Hill "should be used for public enjoyment with particular emphasis upon the interests of young people", and as a Country Park access is available at all times to all people. It had from medieval times been open common land, part of the Duchy manor of Climson (Climsland), and throughout the 20th century was regarded as an open wilderness available for responsible visitors to enjoy, the Duchy helping tarmac the old mine track to the summit in 1928, mainly for the use of pleasure vehicles.

Local people in particular have great affection for the Hill, not just because they take picnics, pick whortleberries, walk their dogs, love the spectacular views across rich farmland to Dartmoor and Bodmin Moor and down the Tamar to the estuary at Plymouth, but also because the Hill is such an important element in their lives. Looming over the district, the Hill's bulk is reassuringly permanent yet its constantly changing heathy surface, greening, flowering, dying back, is excitingly transient. The mass, or mess of archaeological remains is a poignant reminder that their ancestors came up the Hill to work, and to work hard.

An Estates Officer, supported by a Ranger and volunteers, is responsible for the day-to-day management of Kit Hill and ensuring visitors can fully enjoy the openspaces. For further information about Kit Hill, Contact Kit Hill Office, Clitters, Callington, PL17 8HW. Telephone 01579 370030

Main vehicular access is from the east, off the link road between Monkscross on the B3257 and the top of Silver Valley on the A390. You can also park at the foot of the incline on the north side, by the B3257.

Horseriders can enjoy the Hill, using the circular bridle-way and the several short access spurs but the Hill is probably best explored on foot. A waymarked trail connects several of the Hill's most important archaeological sites and vantage points (look out for the distinctive marker stones).

Walkers are welcome to explore Kit Hill but some of the sites descibe in the gazetteer are located away from established paths. Industrial sites are by their very nature potentially hazardous, although shafts and cliff faces are securely fenced. Take great care at all times. Do not climb over fences or into pits, and watch out for adders basking in the sunshine. Treat the Hill with respect and be sure not to disturb the important wildlife.

Kit Hill

In 1967, when this photo was taken, grazing still kept vegetation down, leaving earthworks of mining and quarrying clearly visible. Several close-packed lines of load-back pits (site 11) churn up the ground to the right of the summit mine's stack. The fenced-in North Engine Shaft (see site 17) is visible towards bottom left. Note too the straight line of contiguous prospecting pits (site 8) to the lower right, and South Kit Hill Mine (site 16), with its engine house still standing, in the distance. Two of the enigmatic circular enclosures (site 26) lie beside the sinuous Major Pasture Boundary (site 24).

(Cambridge University AQW 97; Copyright reserved).

A large rounded hill, almost a mountain, climbing steeply for 1000 feet from Luckett to its summit at 1094 feet (334m), Kit Hill is a small outcrop of the great South-Western granite mass rising up between those larger blocks, Dartmoor and Bodmin Moor. The granite intruded as molten rock into sedimentary rocks and the Country Park includes some of these slates on its lower slopes, altered and reddened by the granite's heat. Gases and solutions containing metallic elements found their way into cracks in the granite and slate, and solidified and crystallised into the various ores, notably tin, copper, wolfram and arsenic. These were exploited by miners from at least the medieval period down to the 20th century.

No granite tor survives although an early 19th century map shows one in the area now removed by the large northern quarries (site 23). Instead the movement downhill of rocks and soils in periglacial conditions during the Ice Ages smoothed the Hill's contours. This concentrated weathered tin ore, or shode, eroded from the many lodes coursing east west across the Hill, into the shallow dry valleys, notably the one on the north-east slopes later worked by tin streamers (site 9). Moorstones, blocks of weathered granite, lie scattered on all slopes, including where the bedrock is slate. In places they are so densely concentrated that they can be regarded as clitter.

Although its exposure and altitude mean that it can be very wet, Kit Hill is a 'dry' hill, reflecting its internal domed water table. Springs are few and low lying, and there are no surface streams except for those draining out of the mining adits in the streamworks. The lack of a reliable water supply was to create problems for tinners and miners.

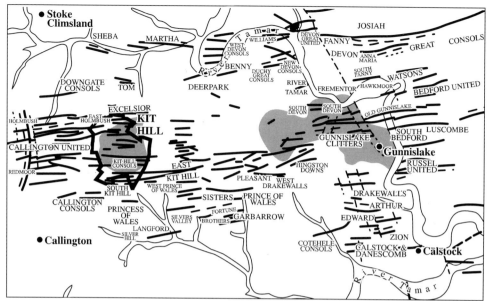

The heart of the Callington - Tavistock mining district showing the two granite outcrops, Kit Hill being the smaller but higher western one, with their attendant lodes and the main mines which worked them (after Dines 1956).

Running away to the east is the ridge of Hingston Down which ends at another granite outcrop above Gunnislake New Bridge. Across this 16th century bridge comes the main road from Tavistock into Cornwall, now the A390, once a turnpike, and before that a medieval thoroughfare. It passed Kit Hill on its southern side on its way to Callington, a small market town snuggling into the Hill's lower slopes and lying on the Launceston to Saltash and Plymouth road (now the A388).

Kit Hill is largely within Stoke Climsland parish but its southernmost corner is shared between Calstock and Callington. A band of 19th century small farms and cottage holdings on the midslopes lies above the more substantial hamlets of Kelly Bray and Downgate, Isacombe and Pengelly.

Kit Hill's surface has been almost completely disturbed by tinners and quarrymen, and thousands of years of grazing has greatly affected soils and plant communities. What appears wild is in fact the typical semi-natural vegetation found on the unenclosed granite uplands of Devon and Cornwall. Walking around Kit Hill is ecologically exhilarating, the site being home to a wide range of flora and fauna, much of which is either nationally rare or under threat and protected by law. Particularly important are the ground nesting birds so please watch out when walking on the Hill.

Wildlife

Field gentians are found at South Kit Hill mine, thriving in soil made alkaline by the lime in the now ruined engine house.

Adders bask in clearings in the bracken. Take care where you place your hands. (Sarah McCartney © Cornwall Wildlife Trust)

Grazing ceased in the 1970s but is being re-introduced to help reverse the recent trend towards European gorse and bracken domination. Although both can look spectacular, the gorse in flower, the bracken as it reddens in the autumn, they crowd out other species and greatly impoverish the wildlife.

It is the Western Heath, with its mix of three species of heather, the low-growing Western gorse, several species of grass and many smaller, often rare plants, which is perhaps the traditional vegetation community on the open top and south-facing parts of Kit Hill. Valuable strips of short acid turf, with sweet herbs, edge this heath along tracks and in well-trodden or rabbit-grazed areas. There will also have been patches of gorse, bracken, and hawthorn and blackthorn as well as areas of purple moorgrass and bents. Trees too have succeeded on the north-facing side and in sheltered spots, in the streamworks and quarries and in the pits and behind the dumps of mine workings. Oak, rowan, holly and, in the damper areas, willow have all matured.

Plants of bog and standing water flourish in the flooded but sheltered quarries and adit entrances and fabulous ferns, mosses and liverworts thrive in the damp calm of abandoned pits, shafts and adits. Lichens, mosses and crevice-growing plants can be seen on old trees and exposed granite.

These habitats support and provide homes for a rich fauna, from insects and spiders to birds, reptiles (including snakes), amphibia and mammals (foxes, badgers, stoats, weasels, rabbits, mice, voles and shrews). You will be unlucky if you don't see either a buzzard soaring or a kestrel hovering and a summer picnic in a sheltered corner can never be taken alone; the creeping and crawling creatures will always want to join in.

The north-western sector of Kit Hill has reverted furthest towards woodland. This part of the Hill is so important for wildlife that it is best left to its permanent residents rather than casual visitors.

People on Kit Hill: Introduction to the Archaeology

People have always come to Kit Hill but they have always left again at the end of the day - from at least the earliest Neolithic period, c 6000 years ago, right through to you. The archaeology, the material remains of people's activities, is the archaeology of a sacred place, a workplace and a playing place; but it is not the archaeology of home. The only remains of dwellings in the Country Park are two ruined 19th century cottages at its extreme southern tip.

There are many interesting ceremonial and recreational sites in the Country Park - a long barrow, several fine round barrows, a peculiar folly, strange circular enclosures - but Kit Hill is most important as an abandoned workplace. In particular the remains of perhaps a thousand years of digging and delving for granite, tin, copper and wolfram make its exploration a journey through the hard, blistered and sweaty lives of scores of generations of Cornish industrial labourers. There are two fully developed tin mines and an unusual

World War One Wolfram Works, but the earlier surface diggings; the streamworks, shode works, stockworks, openworks and lode-back works, form Kit Hill's most valuable metal mining heritage, unique in Cornwall for its intensity. Every known method of granite quarrying, from tiny moorstone pits to the great northern quarries, is also represented on the Hill.

Picking their way through the pits and heaps have always, until very recently, come nibbling sheep and nuzzling cattle, followed by the boys or girls minding them. Grazing leaves little for the archaeologist to record but we can be sure that the total wealth created by turning over virtually the whole surface by miners and quarrymen was only a small fraction of that obtained by six thousand years of quietly pasturing animals.

Prehistoric and Roman Periods
(c 4000 BC to c AD 400)

Exposed to the elements, Kit Hill's summit and higher slopes were probably never forested. Prehistoric herders, from the first farming communities of the Neolithic period (starting c 4000 BC), through those of the Bronze and Iron Ages, and on to those of the Roman period will have sheltered behind some convenient boulder, and surveyed the densely wooded lowlands of East Cornwall. Looking south and east they caught silvery glimpses of the river Tamar winding its way to the sea and away to the west and east they saw the other purple uplands of Bodmin Moor and Dartmoor. Closer to the Hill, maybe even on its lower slopes, they would have seen the smoke rising from their home fires. As the centuries and millennia rolled by the forests were thinned, to be replaced by the farmlands we see today.

The Hill itself was left to the sheep and goats, cattle and horses, and to the children who watched over them.

Surviving prehistoric sites.

- Long barrow
- Kerbed barrow
- Rimmed bowl barrow
- Bowl barrow
- Menhir
- Banks
- Clearance heap

Occasionally people tried to farm here but the place was too marginal. An unfinished field system of Bronze Age type lies on the north-east slopes, its enclosures only partially formed and the ground not fully cleared. Instead the ordinary people only came to the Hill and to the rest of Hingston Down occasionally, for their very important rituals, burials and ceremonies. The place was clearly regarded as special, sacred. Some of their monuments survive.

On Kit Hill's south-eastern slopes is a fine long-barrow (site 1) of Early Neolithic date (before c 3000 BC), used for burial, rituals and ceremonies and probably also marking a territorial claim to at least part of the upland pastures. Serving similar functions are the numerous Early Bronze Age round barrows (c 2000-1400 BC). A long line of these runs along Hingston Down, climbing up to Kit Hill's summit. Eighteen barrows lie within the Country Park although many are poorly preserved, having been damaged by later mining and quarrying (sites 2 to 5 are the best survivors). On the north-west slopes is a naturally upright quartzy stone, possibly used as a menhir or standing stone, another focus for ritual and ceremony.

Medieval (c 400 - c 1550)

Grazing continued. By plotting the known later medieval lowland settlements and their fields we can reconstruct a five-mile long unenclosed block of upland stretching from west of Kelly Bray to the Tamar at Gunnislake. Here the tenants of the great ancient manors of Climson (Climsland), Calstock, South Hill and Calweton (Callington) ran their animals together in the long summer months from May to October.

Most of Kit Hill is within Climson manor (corresponding with the larger part of Stoke Climsland parish) and it must have been groups of tenants of either the Earl or Duke of Cornwall (who owned this manor in the later medieval period) who temporarily enclosed parts of the Hill's west, south and south-east pastures and subdivided them with low parallel banks to form the narrow strips distinctive of Cornish outfields. These were cultivated - the low corrugations of ridge-and-furrow are still faintly visible - but after just

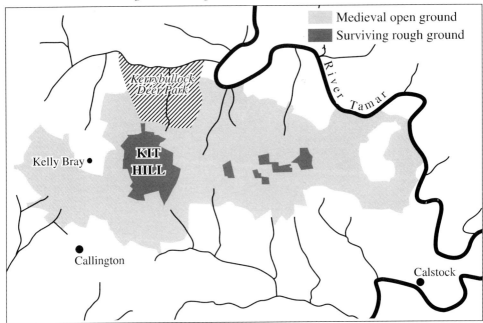

Medieval Hingston Down showing the great expanse of open upland pasture, and Kerrybullock Deer Park (north of Kit Hill). Also shown is the extent of rough ground now left on Hingston Down after post-medieval enclosure - Kit Hill being by far the largest block.

two or three crops, probably of oats and rye, the fences were removed or abandoned and the ground returned to rough pasture.

People and animals skirting Kit Hill on its south side formed deep hollow-ways over the centuries (site 6).

Industrial

Tinners and quarrymen probably began to exploit Kit Hill and the rest of Hingston Down in the later medieval period. The remains of their workings, the streamworks, shodeworks and stone-splitting pits, are introduced separately below.

The slopes of Kit Hill teem with the archaeological remains of industry, but with the exceptions of the summit and South Kit Hill mines and the great northern quarries, this is not the typical stuff of Industrial Archaeology. Few buildings and structures survive and, again with the exception of the northern quarries, no really massive earthworks. Yet there is no question that Kit Hill contains industrial remains of national importance and very wide interest.

It may best be termed landscape industrial archaeology; thousands of features, many interconnecting, are scattered across the whole Hill. The remains are exceptionally well-preserved, there being very little 20th century damage, and they are remarkably wide-ranging, including all known forms of tin mining and granite quarrying. Especially well-represented are the medieval and early post-medieval types of surface mining (generally rare now elsewhere in the tin grounds of Cornwall and Devon), and the early 19th century granite working. On top of this is the sheer density of industrial activity; there are pits literally everywhere, every patch of ground having been at least investigated.

Steeply sloping gunnis of openwork pre-dating South Kit Hill Mine (site 16). Note unstable back-filled material above.

Metal Mining

Kit Hill is towards the western edge of the Callington and Tavistock Mining district and is crossed by dozens of narrow mineralised lodes and veins, all running east-west and some very closely bunched, forming stockworks. Tin, wolfram and some copper have all been won from these and in the medieval period tin was also intensively worked as shode. This is the ore dislocated by weathering from the parent lode and deposited in the much more easily excavated subsoil above the bedrock, often washed down into the valleys where it was worked through streaming.

Prospecting

First find your shode deposit or lode. Most early prospecting on Kit Hill was done by inspecting soil profiles in a series of small pits dug in loose lines running across the east-west lodes. Later they learnt to avoid missing lodes, first by digging lines of contiguous pits and then long costeaning or prospecting trenches exposing stretches of the bedrock (see site 8 for details).

The Archaeology of Kit Hill   **9**

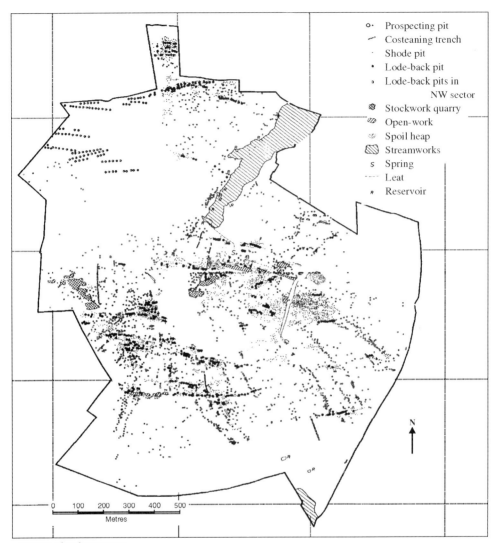

Remains of surface tinning.

In the modern period, the late 18th to 20th centuries, most prospecting was done wholly underground. Adits running north-south into the hillside not only drained the deep mines and provided access, but also allowed the miners to inspect new ground. Cross-cuts, passages driven horizontally at right angles to working levels, and boreholes, were also used.

First the shode....
Concentrated by water action and gravity, the weathered lode, or shode, was exploited by early tinners either in streamworks or in 'shambles' of small pits. (It would also be collected from the upper parts of those later surface workings directed principally at the lodes.)

Streamworkers directed a flow of water through a tye or channel excavated into the shode deposit to separate the very heavy tin ore from the much lighter waste which was taken off in suspension. A well-preserved streamworks, probably medieval, survives on the north-eastern slopes (site 9). At least ten reservoirs holding spring and rainwater brought here by leats (artificial water channels) were arranged around and inside a deep, broad cutting. Spoil dumps within it were thrown up by the streamers and formed sides of the tyes; their carefully planned layout illustrates the streamers' engineering skills as the angle of slope within a tye helped control the rate of water flow, ensuring that all waste was removed, but none or very little of the tin.

On the higher ground, especially on the summit plateau, where water was not available in sufficient quantities to operate streamworks, the tinners worked the shode dry by digging shambles, extremely dense clusters of small pits (site 10). The shode-bearing ground had to be removed downhill to a water supply for dressing before it, along with the streamer's shode, went off to the local blowing-house, for smelting and casting into ingots. Once tested for quality (assayed) by the local Stannary, and after the Duchy had taken its due, these were sold.

....Then the lode

Once economically workable deposits of shode had been exhausted, probably in the 16th or 17th centuries, tinners on Kit Hill became miners and turned their attention to the lodes, picking, chiselling and fire-setting their way into the granite and metamorphosed slate. At first they worked from surface onto the backs of the lodes. Several openworks, long narrow trenches, survive (site 12) but there are many more strings of lode-back pits (site 11). These closely spaced primitive shafts were arranged along a lode and interconnected by underground levels. Spoil had to be hauled out of each openwork and lode-back pit and both sorts of working have irregular heaps to 3 or 4 m high along their sides.

No early tin mill exists on Kit Hill and it seems that the ore-bearing rock was removed from the Hill for dressing, perhaps to the crazing and stamping mills in Kerrybullock Park, a mile to the north. Dressing during this period involved spalling (breaking the stones into small pieces) by hand and stamping (crushing these to a fine powder in a water-powered mill), before separating the tin from its waste.

Probably later than the openworks and lode-back pits are the unusual stockwork quarries on the western slopes and the summit plateau (sites 13 and 14). These irregular, flat-bottomed cuttings were formed, possibly in the early 19th century, by miners removing all the ground containing the many narrow mineralised veins of a stockworks. Again the material was transported off the Hill for dressing.

Into the darkness

Before the days of the earliest deep shafts of the 16th, 17th and 18th centuries, the sky had always been there, right above in an openwork or a stockwork, casting indirect light in a lode-back pit. Now the men were really going underground, candles providing scanty, flickering illumination in the dripping tunnels and jagged stopes; home was a world away.

On Kit Hill the first deep mines were based on adits driven into the shady northern slopes. Gently sloping tunnels, these both drained and gave access to the workings. Several ventilation shafts would be forced up from them and side levels run off east and west to work any good lodes intersected. From the late 17th century gunpowder speeded their excavation. Two such adits were driven in from the floor of the streamworks, and Shallow

North Engine Shaft, the summit mine's major shaft (site 17).

Adit (site 15) may have been first opened long before the 19th century mines it was later to serve.

Later, in the 19th century on Kit Hill, but as early as the 17th in some Cornish mines, mechanised pumping brought water up to adit level and allowed mines to work down to considerable depths. North Engine Shaft at the summit mine (site 17) eventually reached 110 fathoms, or 660 feet (201 metres). The first known mechanical pumps on the Hill were driven by a wind engine built at the summit in the 1820's, which kept dry a shaft sunk to 30 fathoms (180 feet, 55m). Sporadic deep workings, only occasionally successful, continued at the summit and South Kit Hill Mine (sites 16 and 17), the Hill's two fully developed mines, through to the 1880s.

Both sites include a ruined engine house and a prominent chimney stack as well as the other components of Victorian tin mines. Neither mine ever flourished, despite well-publicised and highly optimistic openings and re-openings. The cause was essentially the lack of really rich tin lodes, but poor management and the general collapse of the Cornish metal industry in the face of cheaper foreign imports were also involved in the final shutdown of the mines in 1882 (South Kit Hill) and 1885 (summit). Scores of men had been employed and closure of Kit Hill's mines, along with those at Redmoor and Holmbush in the 1890s greatly depressed the Callington and Kelly Bray area.

Kit Hill is unusual in having several 20th century mines. Most important was the Duchy-run wolfram and tin works on the higher eastern slopes (site 19), opened in 1916 to produce metal for the war effort, and continuing in operation until 1921. Based on levels driven into the hillside, this enterprise also re-worked the summit mine's North Engine Shaft and fruitlessly investigated the abandoned shafts of another earlier 20th century mine on the north-west slopes. This little mine, which worked the rich Quarry Lode and now comprises just two ruined buildings, an adit and several overgrown shafts, was unromantically called No 2 Adit Cross-cut. It was worked from 1902 to 1904 by the Kit Hill Mining Company during one of the Cornish mining industry's quietest periods and was, surprisingly, the Hill's most successful mine. Its brief flowering was even hailed as the Bonanza of the Calstock District, and its profits outstripped those made by either of the Hill's great 19th century mines.

No documentation survives for Jack's Shaft, another late small mine on the north-east slopes (site 18), nor for the tiny overgrown dressing floor in the base of the streamworks. Both appear to have been very small-scale, possibly even single-man ventures, and they provide a fitting end to the story of the often unconventional, sometimes desperate and usually unsuccessful attempts to make a living, never mind a fortune, from Kit Hill's numerous but frustratingly thin metal-bearing lodes.

Granite quarrying

Kit Hill and eastern Hingston Down are two small islands of granite in a sea of slate; Dartmoor and Bodmin Moor are several miles off. Demand for the strong durable stone, used widely in buildings and around the farms, mines and towns of the busy Tamar Valley and Callington areas, was such that these two hills were quarried as intensively as any in

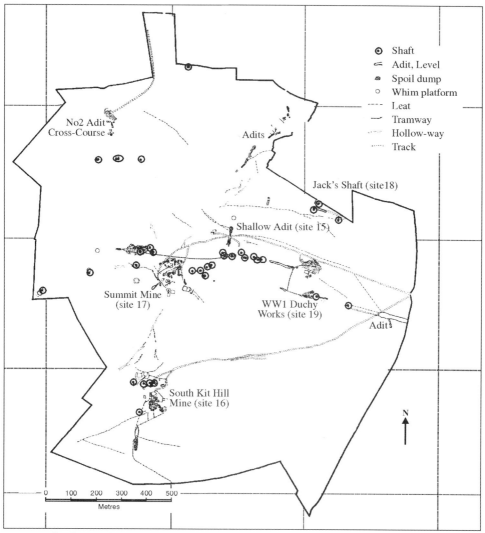

Remains of underground mining and associated features.

the South-West and Kit Hill contains good examples of all the various types of granite quarrying.

Until the 19th century when the use of plug-and-feather splitting and the improvement in controlled blasting techniques enabled commercial granite quarrying to develop, the rock was split relatively casually from the thousands of loose boulders or moorstones on the hillslopes by masons and farmers, miners and millwrights (see site 20).

By the 1810's people were starting little quarrying businesses on the Hill, probably mainly as one-man bands. Scores of the small pits they cut into the bedrock and which would have each yielded hundreds of blocks survive; the early industrial quarries (site 21).

Within a few years, proper industrial quarries were using black powder for blasting and employing large numbers of men and boys. A group of three such quarries on the high southern slopes (site 22) was abandoned early, probably around 1872 while they were still in a fairly primitive form. It seems from their dumps that these quarries, very important archaeological sites now, were mainly producing building stone for local use, including in the mine buildings on Kit Hill itself. Structures in the summit mine for example, including the wind engine and the later chimney stack (1858), would almost certainly have come from them. Metalled tracks running away to the south-east show, however, that most of the stone left the Hill. Look for it in Callington's Victorian houses and shops.

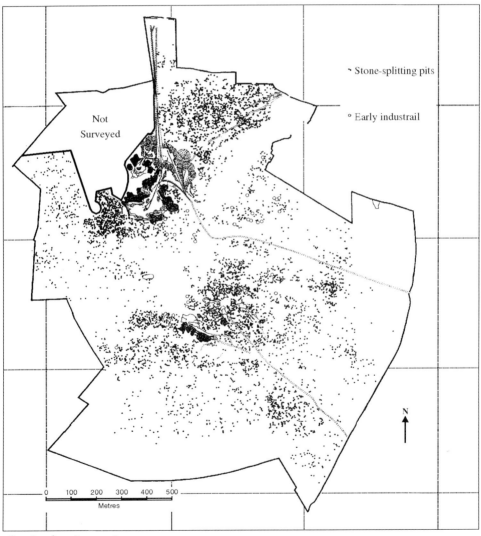

Remains of granite quarrying.

The two great northern quarries (site 23) belong to a whole new industry. They may well have started by supplying the same local building-stone markets as the three southern quarries, but by the last quarter of the 19th century they were producing precisely cut, shaped and finished blocks for civil engineering projects and mighty monuments. Markets were no longer local but national, even international. A fine inclined tramway running down the north slopes got their product onto the East Cornwall Mineral Railway (opened in 1872) which carried it, via another incline, to Calstock's quays. Ships took it to London, where many of the famous bridges and docks are built of Kit Hill granite, and to more distant customers, some as far away as Singapore.

Stones dressed at the northern granite quarry (site 23) for Battersea Park wall (1951) but rejected and left un-used.

The quarries themselves are also quite different in their layout. Flawless granite was found deep in the Hill and great pits (now drowned) were excavated. Cranes hoisted out the blocks and moved them along internal tramways to the dressing floors where mechanical saws and polishers shaped and finished the stones according to the customers' specifications. Only a tiny proportion of the excavated stone eventually left the quarries; the rest, about 90%, was waste and was trammed onto the gigantic finger shaped dumps spreading onto the hillside below. A little of the waste stone was used in manufacturing memorials and paving slabs in the rows of stonemasons' sheds lining the quarries' internal tramways. A second inclined tramway was built exclusively for the larger upper quarry when the smaller pit closed around the turn of the 20th century and by the time the quarry closed in 1955, lorries were sharing the transportation work with the rail network.

Post-medieval (non-industrial)
(c 1550 to the present day)

The archaeology of post-medieval Kit Hill is overwhelmingly that of the remains of mining and quarrying (see Industrial). Amongst the pits, dumps, leats and trackways, however, there are several other interesting sites.

As before, land use was dominated by grazing but now, because of early modern (18th century) attempts to enclose blocks of previously common ground, we can see this form of agriculture clearly through the archaeology. Long stock-proof boundaries formed large irregular enclosures, the most ambitious being that termed the Major Pasture Boundary (site 24) which split the Hill into two unequal parts. Later, in the 19th and 20th

Looking east from Kit Hill along the ridge of Hingston Down. Completely open in the medieval period, this was almost entirely enclosed by straight sided fields in the 19th century.

centuries, piecemeal enclosure of the lower and middle slopes into straight-sided fields gradually reduced the area of rough grazing and left us with the shape of the present Country Park. Small farms, smaller holdings and many cottages were established during this wave of colonisation, largely stimulated by the industrialisation of the Callington-Calstock region, and which saw Hingston Down, with the exception of Kit Hill, almost entirely enclosed and improved. The ruined pair of workers' cottages called Bush Cottages, on Kit Hill's south side, belong to the mid 19th century.

Kit Hill's summit, visible throughout east Cornwall and with panoramic views from it, was put to special use. Since 1929 a Midsummer Eve bonfire has been lit by the Old Cornwall Society, on or near the site of a Tudor and early modern beacon (site 7). In the late 18th century a powerful local landowner, Sir John Call, built what we would now call a folly, a five-sided enclosure (site 25) intended to imitate a Saxon or Danish fort and thus commemorate the battle of Hingston Down, fought nearby in AD 838, which brought an end to Cornwall's independence. A trio of enigmatic circular enclosures (site 26) of similar date on the higher western slopes may be related to Sir John's folly.

Scattered around the Hill, mainly at or near the edges of the Country Park, are a number of 19th century boundstones, all granite and most with carefully inscribed letters or figures, recording the manor, sett or allotment demarcated (see site 27).

Kit Hill summit c1900 from within the folly, showing the engine house (rear right) and other ruined mine buildings. Note the cow grazing peacefully amidst the relics of once vibrant industry. (Kind permission of the Royal Cornwall Museum).

Gazetteer of selected sites

It is not possible in a guide of this size to describe all the sites on Kit Hill. A selection has been made to enable you to visit and appreciate the best preserved and historically most important. Some site types, such as prospecting pits, lode-back workings and stone-splitting pits, have hundreds or even thousands of examples scattered all over the Hill and the gazetteer can only present a general description and discussion. The accompanying map (centre pages) gives locations of particularly good examples.

For a complete description of all sites, see the main report on Kit Hill's archaeological remains published by Cornwall Archaeological Unit (Herring and Thomas 1990).

Some of the sites identified are located away from established paths. Remember that Kit Hill is an old industrial site so take great care at all times. Good walking boots, trousers and waterproofs are recommended. The fencing around features is there for your safety so please do not climb over.

1. Long barrow

Prehistoric

Just inside the Country Park's south-eastern boundary is the oldest archaeological site, an impressive ritual and burial mound of the Early Neolithic period (c 3000 BC), the time of the first farmers. Trapezoidal in plan, with traces of a shallow quarry trench (providing the mound's earth and stones) running along its uphill long side, it is orientated with its wider, business end slightly north of east. There were probably one or more mortuary chambers here, now damaged by the grave robbers who turned this end into a mess of pits and heaps. Some of the large stones scattered around may have come from such a structure. This would probably have housed the often incomplete skeletons of several individuals whose bodies had been first left elsewhere to decay (perhaps also exposed to scavenging by wild animals), before being securely placed within the mound.

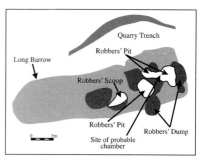

Neolithic long barrow (site 1)

Long barrows were carefully designed with facades around the entrances to the chambers. Here people could gather to perform or witness now unknowable rituals, some of which were clearly related to death, and presumably the worship of spirits and the community's ancestors. It is likely, however, that while long barrows such as this one on Kit Hill housed the dead, their most important functions related to the living community. The labour to build this 40m long, 1.4m high mound would have been communal, drawn from the population around Hingston Down. Once in place the monument would be a powerful territorial marker confirming the community's attachment to a block of land, perhaps the valuable upland pastures running from Kit Hill to Gunnislake. The gatherings at the long barrow,

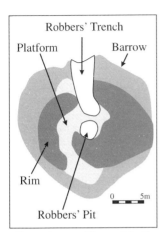

Bronze Age round barrow (site 2).

for burials and perhaps also at other regular times during the year, brought the community together again, reinforcing the commitments of members to each other and to their land.

2. Barrow

Close to the road, about 50m inside the main eastern entrance is one of the Hill's larger round barrows (Earlier Bronze Age, c 2000-1600 BC), a member of the straggling linear group of at least thirty which runs along the length of Hingston Down and over the summit of Kit Hill. Two more, now grassed over, can be seen in the field opposite the entrance to the Country Park.

The barrow is roughly circular (22m diameter, 1.2m high) with traces of a rim bank running around the edge of a fairly flat platform. This is most clear on the west side where there is less damage from robbers' pits and dumps. A crude trench running into the barrow from the north may be an antiquarian's excavation, perhaps from the Victorian period when the inquisitive spent happy Sundays opening local barrows. We now know, from more scientific excavations elsewhere in Cornwall, that the area of Bronze Age activity would have extended out to the very edges of the site, not just confined to the centre. The mound itself was a kind of sealing layer deliberately obscuring the remains of dark and strange rituals; circles of posts, stones or walling, pits with votive offerings, scatters of domestic rubbish, and sometimes, but not always, burials.

3. Barrow

A large simple Earlier Bronze Age round barrow, 21.5m in diameter, 1.0m high, on the summit plateau 35m south-west of the ruined magazine (see site 17). A few stone-splitting pits have nibbled into its edges but the barrow is otherwise in reasonable condition with a good rounded profile. It is part of the same linear barrow group as site 2 and would have been used in the same way.

4. Kerbed barrow/horse-whim platform

An interesting Earlier Bronze Age barrow on the higher western slopes; the only one on Kit Hill whose mound had a retaining kerb. Large slabs of granite on edge survive to the south and west and are detectable through the pits left by their robbers in the north-west. They form more than half a circle whose original diameter was 15.5m.

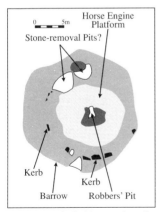

Bronze Age kerbed barrow (site 4) with modern horse engine platform superimposed.

Set on top of the barrow is a horse-engine platform probably dating to the last two or three hundred years. It is level and circular, 11m in diameter with steep-sided edges 0.4 to 0.7m high. An irregular depression in the centre is probably the pit created by those who removed the melior or bearing stone. The horse engine's vertical axle rotated in a small hole drilled into this stone and the machine probably wound material from a nearby shaft.

5. Pair of barrows

On the southern slopes, just within the Country Park's boundary, are two large Earlier Bronze Age round barrows, 85m apart. Standing out well from the moorgrass in an otherwise fairly featureless corner of the hill, they are the most easily appreciated barrows on Kit Hill. As they are about 600m south of the main Hingston Down linear group they appear to be separate from it.

The western barrow, flat-topped, 25m diameter and 2.5m high, is only slightly spoilt by a central robber's pit and a peripheral stone-splitting pit. The eastern barrow (22m diameter, 2.0m high) has a rim bank similar to that at site 2 curving around a platformed mound.

The eastern barrow of the pair on Kit Hill's southern slopes (site 5).

6. Hollow-ways

Medieval

Upland ridges such as Hingston Down have always made good routeways, allowing travellers to avoid the ups and downs of valley sides. On Kit Hill's lower south-eastern slopes, within the Country Park, are several parallel hollow-ways, tracks whose continued use, often over centuries, has eroded deep gullies into the subsoil. These run roughly east-west, following the contour and skirting the highest ground.

One hollow-way saw particularly heavy use. Now overgrown and presumably partly silted up, it still reaches 8m wide and 2m deep; a tall person would have been lost from sight walking along it. This track, on the same contour as the narrow neck of the ridge at Sevenstones, to the east of Kit Hill, veers away north-westwards from the main road to Callington and heads for Kelly Bray and the villages along the east side of Bodmin Moor.

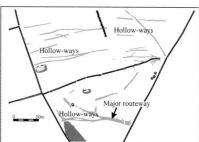

Medieval and early post-medieval hollow-ways (site 6) surviving on the south-eastern slopes.

The Archaeology of Kit Hill **19**

7. Bonfire and beacon

Every year on Midsummer's Eve a bonfire is lit on the levelled platform immediately west of the Summit's folly enclosure (site 25) and a short ceremony, half Christian, half pagan, is performed in Cornish. This is a tradition revived and redesigned in 1929 by the Old Cornwall Society but which has its roots in pre-Christian times. A summer solstice bonfire was just one of several festivals celebrated at various times through the year by the local farming population. Spirits of nature - fire, water, earth and air - were called up and addressed, appealed to and thanked, the people's lives being closely tied up with the natural world. The Church wisely absorbed many of these festivals into its system of rituals, adapting the midsummer bonfire to commemorate the Eve of St John. Sadly, this became one of the victims of the 18th and 19th century erosion by sober local authorities of boisterous rural traditions. There can be little doubt that even the christianised festival was a wild affair.

Midsummer Eve bonfire (site 7) (Steve Scoffin).

Kit Hill, the highest point in east Cornwall, also supported an official beacon in Tudor and early modern times, one of a chain on prominent hills lit to signal danger, to pass information rapidly across country, and to muster levies and militia.

Industrial Metal Extraction

8. Prospecting Pits and Costeaning Trenches

Kit Hill, as anyone who has left the established footpaths well knows, is heaving with small pits, even forgetting for a moment the openworks, shafts and adits and the great granite quarries. An apparently chaotic mix, some were dug by miners as prospecting pits seeking tin lodes or shode deposits, others as the shode pits (site 10) from which were removed quantities of the tin ore weathered from the lodes. Others were dug by local quarrymen, these being the small stone-splitting pits (site 20).

Once carefully surveyed, patterning can be detected which allows prospecting and shode pits to be distinguished and separated. Prospecting pits are usually recognisable as small circular, oval or rectangular pits up to c 2.5m across and now less than 1.3m deep. These have downhill spoil heaps to c 1.2m high, arranged in untidy lines running across the east-west lode lines. Good examples stand out clearly on the lower south-eastern slopes of the Country Park.

Prospectors mainly operated in the early years of Kit Hill's mining history as later tinners needed only to observe the locations of earlier workings to find the lodes. Skill was involved in prospecting. The sides of a pit dug down to bedrock were carefully inspected and the position of any layers of shode studied - the lower down the soil profile they were, the nearer the lode. The next pits, working uphill and thus towards the lode, would be expected to contain more shode and give a better idea of the likelihood of success until eventually a pit was dug which revealed the parent lode on its floor. Kit Hill's geology with its numerous closely packed lodes required particularly sensitive prospecting methods as several layers of shode would be seen within each pit.

Gradually the Hill's miners adopted or developed new prospecting techniques. Some pits were unusually long or cigar-shaped (examples on the south-west slopes) while others were joined together, the long straight rows of touching pits leaving no ground uninspected (fine example on the higher western slopes). A natural progression from conjoined pits was the long trench exposing a considerable length of bedrock. Several of these costeaning trenches, with banks of spoil along one or both sides, survive on Kit Hill. Most can be shown to be relatively early (before the major 19th century mines), but one, the most dramatic, slicing across the higher eastern slopes and probably excavated by machine, was cut during the First World War to search for tin and wolfram lodes (see site 19).

9. Streamworks

Kit Hill possesses one of Cornwall's finest medieval industrial sites east of Bodmin Moor in this extensive streamworks running down the virtually dry valley on the north-eastern slopes. It takes the form of a broad sinuous cutting, between 40 and 100m wide, 1 to 8m deep. In its bottom are complex patterns of spoil dumps, drainage channels and several internal reservoirs. These stored the water used in the key process of separating tin ore (cassiterite), from waste.

Streamers, or tinners, sought shode. The natural sorting it had undergone often produced richly concentrated deposits. The preliminary weathering from the lode saved the tinners the expensive and dangerous job of excavating

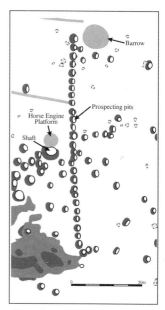

Line of contiguous prospecting pits (site 8) on the western slopes running north-south across main east-west lodes.

Strings of prospecting pits running down the south-east slopes, roughly perpendicular to the lodes whose lines are made visible by the development of more substantial lode-back pits.

Streamworks (site 9) on the north-eastern slopes.

through the host granite. Streamed tin was also more economic to dress and smelt, due to its greater cassiterite content. Most of the earliest tinworks in Cornwall and Devon are therefore streamworks.

By running a stream of water across the deposit of shode the tinners exploited the heaviness of tin by washing off the much lighter waste (silt, clay, gravel and sand), having previously cleared off the sometimes considerable coverings of overburden (peat, soil, stones etc). They had to take great care that the gradients within their working areas, or tyes, through which the water was run, were such that this was satisfactorily achieved. The flow had to be not so weak it left the waste behind and not so strong it swept the tin away. The angles of the tyes to the sides of the main cutting, delicately adjusted to obtain the optimum gradient, are revealed to us by the patterns of the overburden dumps - each of these formed one side of a tye. The locations of several hundred tyes survive in the Kit Hill works, each a monument to medieval hydraulic engineering.

Water has always been a scarce commodity on Kit Hill. The streamworks' reservoirs stored water brought by leat from a now-destroyed spring at Shallow Adit (site 15), and from rain run-off. In a later re-working, water was, most unusually, re-used from further up the works; seven of the ten visible reservoirs

The broad cutting of the medieval streamworks (site 9).

22   *The Archaeology of Kit Hill*

are internal, built into the sides of the cutting, apparently to re-capture water. Other dams were built within the main drainage channels, again presumably to re-use water. Most of the waste would, however, have made its way down through the streamworks to its foot in the Luckett valley and on into the Tamar, contributing to the silting of the estuary.

Being a sheltered depression, the streamworks now has a dense and beautiful vegetation cover which includes many small trees. Dumps and cuttings are also overgrown and the site has mellowed so much that it now appears wholly natural. It is not easy to imagine the noise made, effort expended and riches earned here six or seven hundred years ago.

10. Shode working

Walkers exploring the higher eastern slopes of Kit Hill will encounter masses of small overlapping pits and heaps, a 'shambles' of shode pits (with later stone-splitting pits interspersed). This is one of the best preserved shode workings in Cornwall. There are other shambles on the Hill (nearly 2000 pits being recorded). This one, however, best illustrates the density of pitting, and thus the amount of effort expended in the 'Dry Warkes' John Leland noticed when he visited 'Hengiston' on his Itinerary some time between 1534 and 1543. Where 'Water Warkes', or streamworks were not feasible, normally because hilltop or plateau locations made it impossible to collect the water necessary for them to operate efficiently, the tinners resorted to simply digging over the shode-bearing ground by hand.

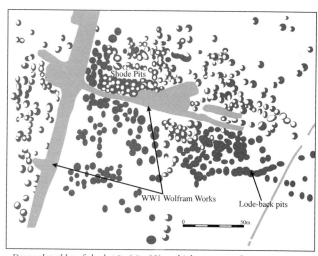

Dense shambles of shode pits (site 10) on higher eastern slopes.

The detailed survey revealed that shode working on Kit Hill was not, as it appears, totally random; the overlapping of pits and heaps showed how the tinners sensibly worked uphill, throwing their spoil downhill onto dead ground, often into the previous days' pits. Once collected the shode would be taken downhill to a ready supply of water for dressing, separating the tin from the waste.

As the tinners would usually have preferred streamworking to dryworking for economic reasons, shodeworks were quite unusual in medieval and early post-medieval Cornwall and Devon. The Kit Hill examples are particularly valuable survivals.

11. Lode-back working

Eventually, probably by the 16th or 17th centuries, tinners on Kit Hill had exhausted the relatively easily obtainable deposits of shode and like tinners elsewhere in South-West England turned to the lodes themselves. This involved excavating into the bedrock, on Kit Hill the granite and metamorphosed slates - work which was much more difficult, time consuming, dangerous and unpleasant and also less certain to bring a return for investment than shode or stream working. In addition more work had to be done on the unweathered ore brought to surface to make it ready for the smelter. It had to be broken down, stamped (crushed) and the tin separated from the unwanted waste rock. Weary, dirty men slipped away from Kit Hill after long, dark, damp days underground.

Lode-back workings on south slopes. Note in particular the long string of pits continuing to the east (right) along the lode later worked as South Kit Hill Mine.

At first, miners must have worked straight onto the backs of the lodes, the surface exposures revealed by prospecting pits and costeaning trenches. On Kit Hill we can see several openworks, long narrow trenches (examples described under sites 12, 16 and 18), but many more lode-back pits, primitive shafts, closely spaced and generally interconnected by underground levels. They are usually 5 to 15m apart, and have wide uncollared openings up to 8m across. Slumped debris and spoil now choke most pits but some on Kit Hill are still open to 6m deep. We do not know their original depths but imagine they went down only as far as was safe, or to the water-table - they do not have

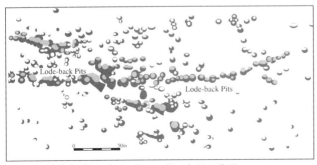

Strings of lode-back pits (site 11) east of South Kit Hill Mine.

24   The Archaeology of Kit Hill

associated drainage adits. Along the line of the lode, the removal of the ore left long narrow caverns. Simple spoil heaps encircle the openings, most of the waste being brought to the surface.

The Country Park contains extremely valuable examples of lode-back working. No less than 41 separate lodes were dug into. The finest run of pits is the 500m long string on the lode later exploited by South Kit Hill Mine (site 16), running east from that mine.

12. Openwork

A short way uphill, to the south-east of Shallow Adit (site 15), is a fenced-in broad gash, one of the best examples of an openwork on Kit Hill. As the name indicates these mines, sometimes dating back to the later medieval period and working directly onto the backs of lodes, were wholly open to the sky, all lode-bearing ground being removed, usually by hand. In this example, which may be no earlier than the 18th century, barrows were used at surface to wheel the spoil onto finger dumps.

Originally c 80m long, the western half was back-filled in the 19th century with spoil trammed from the summit mine's North Engine Shaft (site 17). The surviving eastern half shows how the miners first removed the unstable soil and decayed granite, creating the main cutting c 15m wide, 5m deep. In the floor of this can be seen stretches of the once continuous long narrow gunnis formed by the miners as they followed the lode down through the rock. Most openwork gunnises, which can reach depths of 30m, have become casually filled with debris, and are potentially hazardous sites as this filling is often unstable - hence the fence.

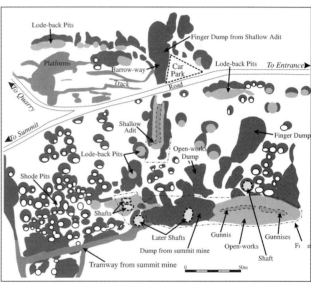

Open work (site 12) and associated dumps, track and buildings. Also shown is Shallow Adit (site 15) and its dump as well as earlier shode and lode-back pits.

A track runs downhill from the area of the openwork to a complex of platforms and very ruined buildings just below the junction of the quarry track and the main summit road. These structures were possibly associated with the openwork, housing smiths and carpenters and other craftsmen working on the mine.

The First World War Duchy mine's No 1 level exploited the same lode and a number of ventilation shafts were forced up through the gunnis (see site 19); two emerge through the North Engine Shaft's dumps.

13. Stockwork Quarries on western slopes

Burrowing into the western slopes are 18 closely spaced irregular cuttings; quarries roughly datable to the early 19th century, which have only minimal dumps. The excavated material was taken from the Hill along three tracks running away to the south-west.

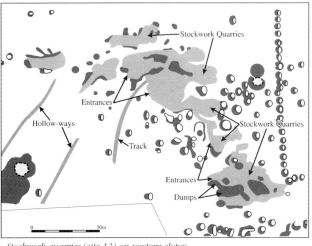

Stockwork quarries (site 13) on western slopes.

Building stone or roadstone may have been quarried here, the metamorphosed shillet either used in the houses of Callington and Kelly Bray, or broken down and used as hardcore on local roads. Neither possibility is, however, very likely as alternative sources could have been easily found much nearer to hand. Instead we should note the orientation of the pits, running west to east into the hillside, along the direction of Kit Hill's tin lodes which are known to have been so closely packed that they were described as "vein swarms" or stockworks. Sometimes it was more economic to work the bunches of narrow veins by excavating all the ground and taking it away to be processed elsewhere, in this case perhaps to the dressing floors of the Callington and Redmoor mines. All the quarries have level floors and downhill entrances wide enough to take a 2m wide vehicle. Lode-bearing rock and shode would have been shovelled from the inner eastern faces straight onto carts backed into the quarries.

Other stockwork quarries exist on Kit Hill, notably to the east of the Summit Mine (see site 14), but this method of mining is fairly rare in Cornwall.

14. Stockwork quarries and shafts east of summit mine

The area at the summit to the north-east of the triangulation pillar contains three old stockwork quarries (see site 13) up to 4.0m deep, with irregular dumps on their floors indicating that some preliminary sorting took place on site. Also of interest is the tramway which passes through all three quarries, stepping down with revetted tipping platforms at two points, turning a tight angle of 85° at another and finally running out onto the fine 4m high finger dump overlooking the summit road. These quarries probably date from the early 19th century. Two of the three summit mine shafts sunk into the floors of the northern two quarries apparently pre-date the final phase of that mine (site 17), as do the two shafts with walls around them immediately to the south and west of the quarries.

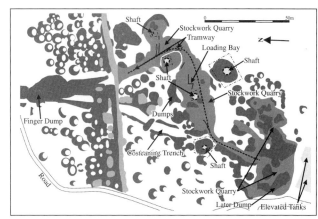

Complex of three stockwork quarries and interconnecting tramway (site 14) to north-east of summit.

15. Shallow Adit

This adit has the summit road passing between its entrance lobby and dump, just 50m before the quarry track branches off. The adit, possibly originally dug in the 17th or 18th centuries as part of a simple shaft and adit mine was later re-used principally for drainage, connecting underground with South Engine Shaft of the summit mine (site 17). It was certainly draining that mine by the mid-19th century and perhaps also during its 1820s-30s workings. The upper, later dump was probably formed during its re-opening in the First World War (see site 19). A tramway or barrow-way is still visible along its back. A horse engine on the circular platform a little way downhill may have wound spoil trucks out onto it.

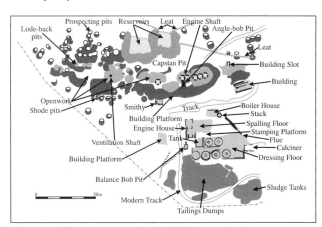

Remains of the central area of South Kit Hill Mine (site 16).

The Archaeology of Kit Hill **27**

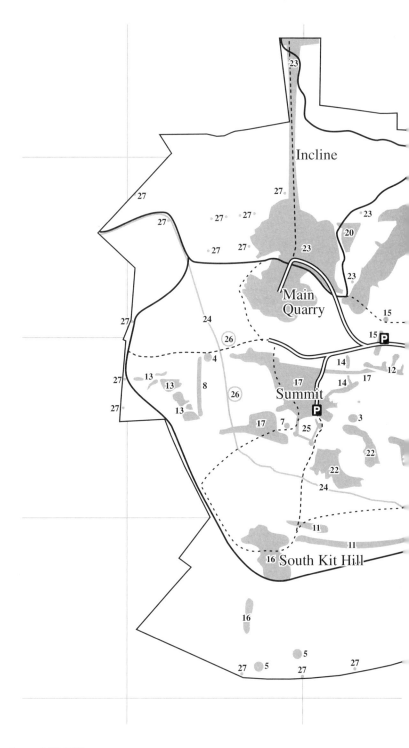

The Archaeology of Kit Hill

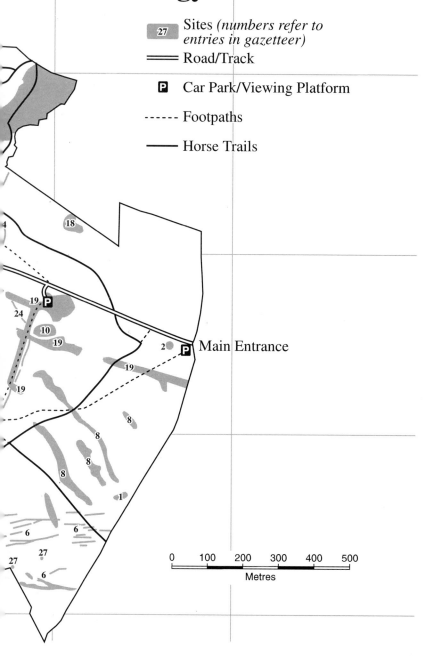

Several leats originated at Shallow Adit, including two which fed the much earlier streamworks (site 9). There is a strong likelihood that a natural spring existed here; the early miners may have forced their adit into this point of weakness.

16. South Kit Hill Mine

Drawing you down or around to the south slopes is an elegant stack, a slender sentinel looking over the stony ruins of South Kit Hill Mine. Here are the remains of a typical 19th century small tin mine with its components close together, well-preserved and reasonably easy to appreciate and understand. Its simplicity is due to its short, fairly unsuccessful history which saw two brief workings. The first, as South Kit Hill Mine, ran from 1856 to 1874. Most activity, however, was concentrated in the last two years. The second was as Cornwall Great Consols (the name following the famous and very successful Devon Great Consols, just across the Tamar) from 1879 to 1882. The mine finally closed after messy legal actions for fraud were coupled with a failure to find good tin in the harder granite after the softer slates had been worked through at the 50 fathoms level. Most of the buildings went up in the earlier working.

South Kit Hill stack (site 16). Note put-log holes from construction scaffolding in the stone-built lower two-thirds. Spalling floor and engine house in background.

Miners were, however, active here long before the 19th century. Several runs of prospecting pits (site 8) climb the Hill and cross the lode at the site's west end where a number of shode pits (site 10) are also clustered. These may be medieval. A few centuries later a long string of lode-back pits (site 11) was opened, stretching fully 500m east to west, and then in the core area a line of four openworks (see site 12) was excavated.

The best openwork gunnis to view at South Kit Hill is the most westerly. It is 39m long, largely infilled with loose rubble which has recently partly subsided revealing that the openwork was created in two stages; the narrow gunnis, 2m wide and dipping to the north, is in the bottom of a broader cutting c 10m wide and 2.5m deep. Undulating spoil heaps up to 3.5m high run along its sides.

South Kit Hill Mine (site 16) in the mid-1970s. View from engine shaft through the ivy-clad angle-bob pit to the now partially demolished engine house. (Adam Sharpe).

It was through another gunnis that the 19th century mine's main engine shaft was sunk. This has a double opening, one side for pumping, one for hauling. Any spoil brought up the shaft was removed through the adit c 100m downhill to the south-west, but how the ore was brought up is still a little uncertain. The steam engine only pumped and stamped and there are no signs of a platform for a horse-powered winding engine. A "drawing-machine" with 100 fathoms of wire-rope was sold at the mine's closure.

This machine was probably housed in a shed (also sold) attached to the north side of the engine-house.

The engine house, first recorded in 1872, contained a steam driven rotary beam engine with a 32-inch diameter cylinder. Its south-facing bob-wall supported the rocking beam which turned, via a sweep arm and a crankshaft, two fly wheels whose stone-lined slots are still clearly visible in the adjoining loadings or platform. These flywheels controlled the power applied to a stamping mill to the east and to the pumps in the shaft. Stone faced pits for rocking bobs are visible at each end of the line along which flat-rods transmitted horizontal movement from the engine to the pumps. Immediately south of the shaft is the pit in which an angle-bob altered the direction of movement from horizontal to vertical, rhythmically lifting and lowering pumping rods in the shaft, forcing water up to the 12 fathoms level and out through the mine's adit. At the flat-rod's other end, just south-west of the engine, is the balance-bob pit in which a beam weighted by a stone-filled box counterbalanced the weight of flat-rods and pumping-rods. This greatly relieved the strain on the engine. A small circular pit north of the shaft contained the capstan used occasionally to haul up the pumping rods and pump parts for maintenance work.

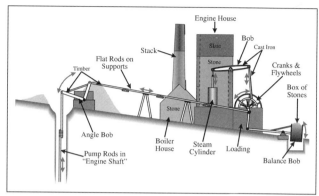

Reconstruction of the pumping arrangements at South Kit Hill Mine, Callington (Nigel Thomas).

Sadly the engine house was partly destroyed in the early 1980s after being declared unsafe. Walls which photographs show once contained neatly arched windows were pushed inwards obscuring internal features. Steam for the engine came from the boiler house whose footings lie immediately west of the chimney; the blocked, brick-arched flue opening can be seen at the stack base.

The engine condensers, boilers, and the dressing floors all required water, scarce on Kit Hill. Shaft water was corrosive so leats were cut on the slopes above the mine to collect run-off rain water and guide it into the two rectangular reservoirs uphill from the shaft.

Once at surface the ore was prepared on site for the smelter. Remains of the several stages of the dressing process are clearly visible at South Kit Hill.

First, on the spalling floor, the lofty paved platform immediately east of the engine house, bal maidens and boys took lumps of ore-bearing stone and spalled (broke) them down with hammers until small enough to be crushed in the stamping mill. The stamps were arranged on the now overgrown lower platform south of the spalling floor. As South Kit Hill Mine prospered in 1872 and 1873 new batteries of stamps were apparently installed here, steadily increasing the number of heads from 12 to 24 to 36. Stamps were vertical timber rods with heavy iron bases, lifted and dropped by cams on a horizontal axle turned by the engine. Chutes fed ore from the spalling floor into boxes containing the batteries of stamps and, with water added, the finely crushed ore left the stamps through grates as a dense red liquid, ready for the separation of the tin from the lighter waste-rock.

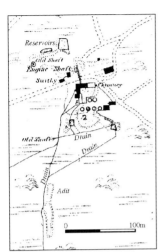

South Kit Hill Mine (site 16). Planned when still operating in 1881 (OS).

After passing through the raised rectangular settling tank to the north-west of the dressing floor, the liquid pulp was fed by wooden launders onto the centres of circular buddles. Slowly revolving brushes spread the sludge over the buddles' concreted central cones while water was trickled across the material. The significantly heavier tin fell out of suspension much more rapidly than the lighter waste which was taken towards the buddles' edges as liquid. This eventually passed down to a pair of slime tanks to the south-east of the dressing floor where fine tin and the lighter waste was settled out to allow relatively clear water to run away from the mine. The buddles were regularly emptied by boys and bal maidens. Unwanted waste, the 'tailings', at the outer edges was barrowed away to the tailings dump, the irregular sandy mound to the south-west (now home to the rabbits whose nibbling helps keep the dressing floors relatively open). The 'heads', the richest tin stuff at the top of the buddles (c 60% pure) were ready for the smelter but the 'middles' were usually re-buddled.

Of the surviving buddles, the western five probably belong to the first working and the sixth to the floor's eastward extension in 1881. Shallow depressions in the south-east corner of the new floor were either further settling tanks or the foundations of other mechanised separating devices. Slots for timbers supporting a roof over the extension survive in its external revetment. Attached to its east side is a ruined rectangular building with a horizontal flue leading to a blocked opening on the east side of the chimney stack. A small calciner was probably housed here; it would have roasted the processed ore to remove arsenic and other impurities.

Other interesting buildings are scattered around the mine. A small smithy, still containing its anvil base, can be found built against the dumps to the south-west of the shaft. There would have been plenty of work for the smith (sharpening drills, making and repairing tools and machines) and for the carpenter and clerk whose workshops were amongst the several other small buildings whose footings survive. Safely 100m away to the east is the now ruined magazine where the mine's explosives were stored.

The footpath running along the Hill's south-eastern slopes from the main road entrance to South Kit Hill Mine re-uses the mine's principal access track. In places slightly hollowed and in others raised onto a low embankment, but always level and of an even width (greater than 2.5m), the track appears to have been roughly metalled, possibly in 1872 specially for the great waggons bringing the heavy parts of the mine's steam engine over the final, most difficult mile.

17. Summit Mine

The summit carpark is in the heart of a mining complex which, although less well preserved and more confused than South Kit Hill Mine (site 16), still contains much of value and interest, not least the remarkable stack.

Earthwork remains of shode and lode-back pits (especially to the west) confirm that tinning has gone on here for many centuries (see sites 10 and 11). The buildings and features on the flat ground between the folly and the little mountain of heaps around North Engine Shaft belong to a series of shortlived, often exciting, but ultimately unsuccessful openings in the 19th century.

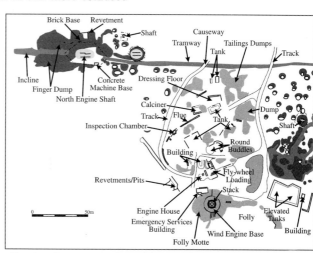

Remains of summit mine (site 17) (core area).

The earliest known mechanised working, under the name Kit Hill Mine (1820s and 30s) saw a wind engine erected over a shaft and made to pump water; its base is still

Kit Hill summit mine complex from the east. Engine house dressing floors, calciner, etc. are contained by the delta of modern tracks. North Engine Shaft is to top right, with its tramway running off to bottom right. The pair of elevated tanks are below the modern carpark. Sir John Call's Folly (site 25) is to the left of the stack.

visible beneath the chimney stack. The 30 fathoms level had been reached when a violent storm in 1836 terminally damaged the engine and the mine closed, all its materials being sold the following year. The auction schedule shows a fully equipped mine with horse engine, dressing floor, smithy, carpenter's shop and count house. None can now be certainly located although the small northern dressing floor with stone-lined settling tanks and low tailings dumps may belong to this early working which raised and sold considerable quantities of tin and copper.

Between re-opening in 1846 and closure again in 1850, an under-financed venture had concentrated on driving adits at various depths (one at 53 fathoms) to drain the workings and to intersect known lodes. Then, some time between 1850 and 1852, the mine re-opened as Kit Hill United. After a few quiet years the purchase of a steam engine was announced in 1857; its house and stack were under construction amid great local optimism - plenty of tin, wolfram and copper being anticipated - and much excitement, especially over the erection of such a large and 'noble' stack. This was still incomplete in May 1858 when the engine was started, "a great day in the modern history of the old mountain"(Mining Journal). When whitewashed, the 83 feet (25m) high stack would double as a landmark at sea. Its decorative design, mimicking an ornamental column, was apparently insisted upon by the Duchy, a plain stack being thought unsuitable for such a prominent position.

Engine house and stack of summit mine (site 17) in c1900 with the boiler revealed by demolition. (Trounson-Bullen Collection; copyright reserved).

Early 20th century demolition has left little of the engine house; only the lowest courses of the bob-wall on which the engine's beam rocked and, to its east, the loadings in which two flywheels turned. Displaced and broken, but still within the house, is the granite bedstone on which the engine's 30 inch diameter cylinder sat. The house may have been beautifully finished - old photos show a classical flat-roofed building with fine arched windows - and the stack may have looked grand, but the mine was still struggling. The overworked engine pumped and hauled from two shafts and operated a set of tin stamps as well as occasionally working a copper crusher.

A pair of elevated stone-faced tanks, one now with the OS triangulation pillar on its corner, probably held water pumped all the way up South Engine Shaft for use in the engine's boiler and condenser and on the dressing floor (with its round buddles and rectangular tanks) to its north. The stamping mill was between this floor and the engine house.

Stretch of the summit mine's calciner flue (site 17).

The stack was also well-used, providing draught not only for the engine's boiler house but also, via a long, curving horizontal stone-lined flue running away 120m to the north, for a calciner or burning house, now a ruined rectangular building. Dressed ore was roasted here in a simple oval furnace until arsenic and other impurities were released as gases which were sucked along the flue towards the chimney only to be baffled by the cross-wall of a small square chamber built part way along. This encouraged the arsenic to settle on the walls of chamber and flue. The fine white crystals would then be periodically scraped off and kept for sale.

South Engine Shaft was the lesser of the mine's two main shafts, being sunk to just 40 fathoms. Away to the northwest is North Engine Shaft, the mine's principal access point, now a gaping hole surrounded by fences. (KEEP OUT! This shaft, the deepest on the hill, was sunk to 110 fathoms, or 660 feet). Flat-rods brought power here for the shaft's pumping rods and presumably cables were also brought from a winding drum to a headgear over it. Spoil hauled to surface was either run away to the east along a tramway cutting and dumped into an old openwork (site 12), or heaped up around the shaft's north and west sides. The strange inclined plane running down the western dumps into a blind cutting may have been used in some way to move trucks around the various finger dumps.

Summit mine (site 17) planned by OS in 1881 at the commencement of its final working.

Some economies are false and the strain on the poor engine eventually broke Kit Hill United as, in October 1864, the cylinder split from top to bottom. Around 100 people lost their jobs when the elderly proprietor closed the mine, which had sold £18,000 worth of tin, wolfram

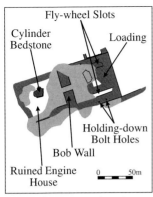

Ruins of summit mine's engine house (site 17).

Contemporary (1832) sketch of the summit wind engine (RIC) (see site 17).

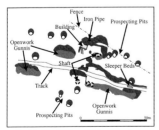

"Jack's Shaft" late 19th or early 20th century mine (site 18) cut through earlier openworks.

and copper. A few attempts to work the adits were made in the later 60s and 70s but the engine was left unrepaired until the final, most frustrating episode in the mine's history, the launching in 1881 of Kit Hill Great Consols Co. Ltd.

The new Company, inspired by the success of Devon Great Consols a few miles to the east, threw itself into a wildly ambitious scheme to connect a deepened North Engine Shaft (then at 62 fathoms) with a proposed extremely deep and spacious adit or tunnel driven into the Hill from its north side. The tunnel, known as the Excelsior, would be used not only for drainage and haulage, but also for locating new lodes. Once the engine had been repaired and the mine drained and thoroughly refurbished, the twin jobs of deepening the shaft to 110 fathoms and driving the tunnel began. Work in the shaft went well but progress in the tunnel was slow and beset with problems. Shareholders began to voice concerns about the lack of returns and the increasingly gloomy prospects as the tunnel failed to find rich lodes. In 1885 they forced the mine's closure with the tunnel 353 fathoms long, but still 247 fathoms short of connecting with North Engine Shaft which had by then reached the desired depth.

Prominent on the plateau east of the summit mine is the surviving south gable wall of a small square building, the mine's magazine or explosives store. Fragments of wood from the four internal shelves can be seen in their slots and a recess on the outside of the wall probably held a plaque warning people away from this dangerous building, situated for obvious safety reasons, over 100m east of the mine. It is not shown on the 1881 OS map so belongs to the last four years of Kit Hill Great Consols working.

18. Jack's Shaft

This tiny mine on the north-east slopes, not shown on the 1881 OS map but extant by 1905, was conceivably worked by a solitary miner. It is labelled 'Jack's Shaft' on the 1920 plan of the World War One Duchy mine (site 19).

Jack was presumably attracted to the site by two lines of much earlier openworks, c 20m apart, and he sank a shaft onto each lode. A small building platform, a few metres west of the blocked northern shaft may have held a winding machine as a stone-lined pit attached to it is aligned with the open, but fenced southern shaft. Work in this southern shaft was more extensive; its dumps are larger and a short tramway, along which trucks were pushed by hand, was laid through the old openwork and onto them. There is no dressing floor and Jack presumably took any ore he raised to a local stamping mill.

19. World War One Wolfram and Tin Mine

A car park has been established on the northern dump of the mine opened in 1916 by the Duchy of Cornwall to work for tin and wolfram as part of the war effort. By 1918, there were 100 men working underground and 70 more at surface and the Duke himself visited the site. After the war, with blockades lifted, the mine struggled and finally closed in 1921.

In January 1916 a massive costeaning trench (see site 8) was cut, probably by machine, across the high eastern slopes and four lodes exposed by it were explored, two very briefly. Another to the north was more promising and substantial quantities of tin and wolfram were obtained as No 1 level was driven west along it to connect with old Shallow Adit (site 15). No 1 level, partially open to the sky, goes underground after c 80 m and several ventilation shafts driven up from it further west are now fenced. The car park is on the substantial dumps created from its spoil. A small concrete count house stood near the level's entrance until recently and a machinery plinth still visible on a concrete building platform to the north may have held a winding machine moving trucks along the working's tramways.

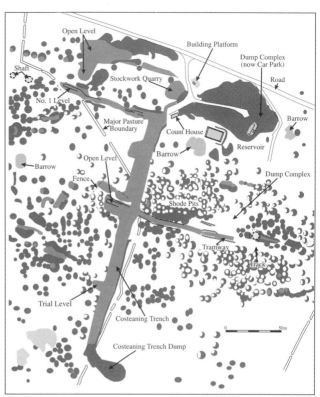

Central part of First World War Duchy wolfram mine (site 19) on higher eastern slopes. No 2 level is downhill to the east.

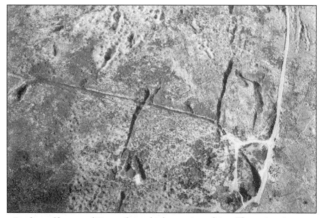

Duchy wolfram and tin works on higher eastern slopes. The costeaning trench runs across the photo with trial and working levels running up into the slope. Bottom right is the complex dump from No. 1 level.

The Archaeology of Kit Hill

Photograph taken during the operation of the wolfram mine (site 19), showing a tipping truck on the tramway (left) and stepped trunk buddles with access staging (right) (Trounson-Bullen Collection; copyright reserved).

Lobby and portal of central exploratory level of First World War wolfram works (site 19).

Those trucks carrying ore were sent halfway along the old costeaning trench to the cutting of the other extensive exploratory level, opened at roughly the centre of the trench. From here can be seen the portal or entrance to this unsuccessful level's short underground part. Ore from No 1 level was tipped into the lobby cutting and sent down a short inclined plane towards No 2 level, the cutting on the Country Park's lower eastern slopes has the remains of the mine's ore hoppers on its extensive dumps still visible in the privately owned field across the road. From these an aerial cableway supported by pylons sent the ore 2.5 miles across country to Clitters Mill near Gunnislake for dressing. No 2 level was intended to intersect the rich south-dipping lodes worked in No 1 level and to connect with winzes (internal shafts) sunk from that level; ore could then have been hauled straight out of No 2 level, greatly reducing the haulage costs which were crippling the mine. Unfortunately for Kit Hill's miners, history was to repeat itself as time, finances, the hardness of the granite and the relative poverty of the lodes in depth saw this vital level abandoned short of its goal, just as Excelsior's Tunnel's failure had ruined the summit mine in the 1880s (see site 17).

20. Stone-splitting pits

You cannot blindly crash about on Kit Hill; there are pits everywhere, in all corners. Miners' pits, with visible heaps, can generally be avoided but most of the 4,839 recorded stone-splitting pits have insignificant heaps or none at all, and are painful traps for the unwary. Such density, greater than on either Bodmin Moor or Dartmoor, is due to the considerable local demand for granite being supplied from a very small area; Kit Hill and eastern Hingston Down. The main local use of granite was in farms, particularly for gateposts, and in buildings, usually strategic lintels, arches, jambs and quoins. It was also shaped, by skilled masons, into millstones, cider and cheese press bases, rollers, troughs and the like.

Stoneworkers mainly exploited 'moorstones', weathered surface stones dislodged from the parent rock. The pits they left are small, yielding less than a dozen usable blocks, and are shallow and angular, with at least one side defined by the unused stone. On this surviving face you may see the splitting marks.

Earliest are wedge marks, some of which will date back at least to the 16th century. Iron wedges were placed into a line of four or five chiselled grooves, each about 12cm long and 7cm deep, and struck in turn by a sledge hammer until the stone split. The chiselling was laborious and the method was abandoned around 1800, on the invention of the plug-and-feather method, possibly by the famous engineer Richard Trevithick. Hand drills were used to create lines of circular holes for the iron plugs, placed between thin iron feathers, which were again successively struck by a sledge hammer. The first drilled holes were fairly thick, c 3cm in diameter, but by the mid-19th century an optimum splitting diameter nearer 1cm was being used.

Some Kit Hill pits display the marks of both methods, drilled holes clearly secondary to wedge marks. Two very interesting examples have alternate wedge and thick drill marks on a single splitting line, showing how innovations are sometimes adopted only cautiously, the stone-splitters mixing the strange new method with the old and familiar.

Kit Hill's stone-splitting pits unusually contain virtually no discarded waste pieces; demand for granite was such that all loose pieces were taken. Relatively few split faces are curving - most have the straight faces left by simple rectangular blocks. There are, however, two abandoned, broken millstones, hidden away on the higher north-western slopes. One, cracked across its centre, was being worked with wedges and is thus quite old, pre-1800.

Granite Quarrying

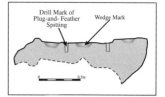

Moorstone to north-east of main quarry dumps with the marks of wedge and plug-and-feather splitting on the same plane (site 20).

Stone splitting pit (site 20). Four holes drilled ready for plug-and-feather splitting run down the left side of an abandoned detached block. The line of six splitting marks along its top match those on the face of the parent moorstone in the background.

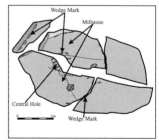

Millstone on north-west slopes abandoned after cracking during manufacture. Wedge-marks indicate a pre-1800 date (see site 20).

21. Early Industrial Quarries

On the north-eastern slopes, east of the streamworks (site 9), is a cluster of tiny granite quarries, each less than 10 m across and no more than 2m deep. Others are scattered over the Hill's higher slopes. They have simple downhill entrances, wide enough to admit a wagon or sledge, and worked exposures of the bedrock, not just moorstones (compare with stone-splitting pits, site 20). Low heaps of the covering earth, or overburden, edge the pits which were large enough to produce hundreds, even thousands of usable blocks. These are rare examples of the earliest industrial granite quarries, dating to the first decades of the 19th century and made commercially viable by the invention of plug-and-feather splitting (see site 20) and the burgeoning demand for granite created by the industrialisation of the Callington-Calstock area.

The erection of the Robinsland boundstones on the north-west slopes (see site 27) followed disputes from 1812 to 1814 between the Duchy and some of its tenants who were attempting to set up quarrying businesses, no doubt in quarries such as these.

22. Southern Quarries

High on the southern slopes, c 75m apart, are three well-preserved fully industrial granite quarries, active into the second half of the 19th century, but unusual in having then closed, not developing into the more mechanised era of the late 19th and early 20th centuries. Their closure may have followed the opening in 1872 on the north side of Kit Hill of the East Cornwall Minerals Railway which ran to Calstock, the Tamar and beyond and gave the two northern quarries (site 23), connected to it by an inclined tramway, a significant commercial advantage. Transport costs were critical in those days and these southern quarries were probably forced to close because they relied on waggons trundling away south-eastwards, down a roughly metalled track.

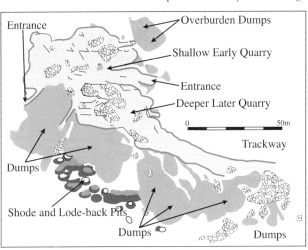

Western-most of three mid-19th century quarries (site 22) on the high southern slopes.

The largest and most convenient to visit is the western quarry, just a few metres south-east of the summit folly. As it deepened towards the south-east, the earliest workings in the north-west, probably dating back to the first quarter of the century, were left high and dry. Overburden dumps here were low and flat-topped. The working faces, their lines following natural east-west cleavage ways, contain both the early thicker drill marks of plug-and-feather splitting, and the relatively short circular-sectioned early charge-holes, drilled to take the explosives used to dislodge larger blocks of granite.

As the later south-eastern part reached depths of over 4m, its access became confined to the narrow channel carved out of its bottom end. Dumps here were also larger, reaching 7.5m high, and tend to be more finger like, trucks having trammed waste along temporary rails to be tipped over their ends.

23. Northern quarry complex

The Hill's most dramatic archaeological site: two major granite quarries with enormous dumps and steep inclined tramways running down to Downgate Sidings on the old East Cornwall Minerals Railway (ECMR).

The southern quarry, at least, opened early in the 19th century, long before the railway came in 1872. The floor of an impressive hollow-way running away from this quarry to the north-east and which was replaced by the incline to the railway, has in places been worn down to over 2m deep by waggons and sledges carrying away the heavy granite.

You are encouraged to explore the larger, more interesting southern quarry and to leave the marshy and overgrown northern one,

Northern quarry complex showing both pits, the overburden dumps, waste dumps and the top of the later incline.

abandoned by 1905, to the wildlife which thrives in its damp and sheltered habitat. Regular blastings, clouds of dust, the screaming of cutting and dressing machines, the busy movement of cranes, trucks and lorries, and of course the murmuring and shouting of scores of workmen could all be seen and heard in the southern quarry as recently as 1955, the year of its closure. See how quickly nature has softened this the harshest of industrial sites.

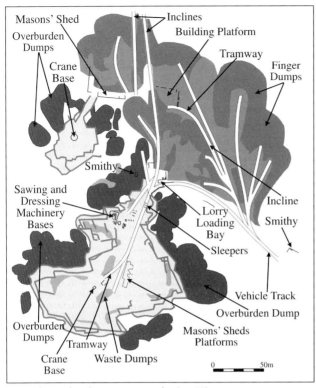

Central part of northern quarry complex (site 23).

At first the floor of the quarry was kept on the level as it ate its way southwards into the hillside. A fairly shallow pit, now waterfilled, was dug in the south-east corner before attention was turned to the south-west. The lake here is as deep (13m) as the cliffs above it are high, the finest flawless granite being found at depth. Pumps kept the pit dry, the water being piped to the dressing sheds for cooling saws and dampening down the lethal dust. Large blocks were carefully eased from the quarry face by highly skilled, almost delicate use of black powder explosives. Quarrymen made good use of the granite's natural horizontal cleaving ways; you will see their long charge holes in the cliff-faces.

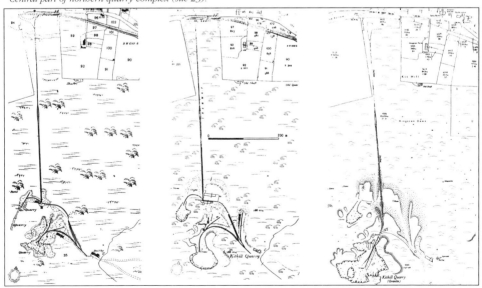

These OS plans of 1881, 1905 and 1951 illustrate clearly the development of the quarry complex (site 23). Note the early 20th century abandonment of the smaller quarry and the consequent replacement of its inclined tramway.

Granite from these quarries was excellent stuff, being used in major civil engineering works including six London bridges (Lambeth, Putney, London, Blackfriars, Chelsea and Waterloo), the Thames embankment and the docks at Millwall, Tilbury and Devonport and overseas at Gibraltar and Singapore. Hanois lighthouse (Guernsey) and the outer skin of Bishop's Rock lighthouse (Scilly) also came from here. Such works required very large blocks of clean granite, precisely cut and perfectly finished, no error allowable. Stone dressers served several years apprenticeship. In the 19th century much work was done by hand using hammers and chisels. Sawing, shaping and polishing machinery, powered first by oil engines and then by electricity, was installed in large corrugated iron sheds within the southern quarry in the early decades of the 20th century. Their concrete floors and concrete plinths, for the engines and the machines they drove, survive. Earlier dressing sheds, extant by 1905 and serving both quarries, stood at the rear of the level platform made on top of dumps to the east of the incline; some footings survive.

Early 20th century quarry workers (by kind permission of Callington Musuem).

Cranes and tramways moved the granite. Still visible under water in the lake is the square foundation block with four bolts which held a fixed crane hoisting blocks out of the pit. Traces of earlier fixed cranes can also be found, lengths of anchor chains high in cliff faces or anchor rings on rocks beyond the quarry's edge. The northern quarry has a central circular crane base. Other cranes were mobile, carrying blocks along tramways to the dressing floors and to the long lines of stonemasons' sheds which turned out thousands of gravestones and paving stones.

The great northern granite quarry (site 23).

Less than 10% of the excavated rock was actually used; the other 90% was waste, either flawed or discarded as trimmings when blocks were reduced to required shapes. Lumps of waste could weigh several tons and they were crow-barred in trucks along the narrow gauge tramways running out along the backs of the massive finger dumps (up to 14m high) and tipped over their ends. Impressions of the wooden sleepers in these temporary tramway beds can still be made out. More permanent tramways had granite sleepers or setts; some can be found along the

Finished granite awaiting delivery to customers (by kind permission of Callington Musuem).

The Archaeology of Kit Hill **43**

Northern granite quarry (site 23); the later incline runs down to Downgate sidings to the right while a tramway bed runs onto a waste dump to the left.

present quarry access track, the level bottom part of which was once a tramway taking waste to the main eastern dumps and cut stone to a short inclined tramway running down to the early dressing floors on the flat platform, and also to the top of the earlier incline.

The top of this early incline, probably built in 1872 to connect with the ECMR, was to the east of the lower northern quarry, it being more economic to bring stone down to the incline from the higher quarry than up from the lower one. At a central passing bay the descending truck, at one end of a cable, swayed past another pulled up at the cable's other end. A cable drum shed and a small turntable, connecting the internal quarry tramways with the incline, which also had narrow gauge tracks, are shown on early OS maps at the incline top but their sites are unfortunately now lost, buried beneath a 10m high heap of waste from the upper quarry. To form an even plane on an uneven hillside, the incline builders made cuttings at top and bottom and supported the central portion on an embankment of waste boulders.

Northern granite quarry (site 23). Ruined magazine.

After the northern quarry's abandonment, probably in the first decade of the 20th century, transportation of stone from the southern quarry to the incline via several internal tramways became unnecessarily expensive. A new incline was built, which came up to the level of the quarry's entrance. Its rails were standard gauge, compatible with the railway at its foot. Here the incline forked, one line going into the sidings, the other to a safety buffer stop, now a mound of earth, which prevented runaway trucks from careering onto the railway. A buffer support at the east end of the Downgate sidings survives as do the two well-built heads of a bridge carrying the railway over a passage left open to allow livestock to be driven on and off Kit Hill.

Towards the end of the quarry's life, road vehicles were also being used to take away finished work. The present quarry track was roughly metalled with cobbling, and lorries using it backed into a rectangular loading bay immediately south of the incline's winding shed.

Ancillary buildings include a smithy and two magazines. The smithy, built before 1881, is the long ruined building to the east of the dumps, just below the quarry track. With three main rooms and an annexe to the north, it probably also accommodated the quarry office as well as other craftsmen, including the carpenter. A few metres downhill is a small stone-lined wheelpit, once holding an overshot wheel turned by water brought by leat from Shallow Adit (site 15). It clearly powered machinery associated with the smithy, being operational in 1881. Perhaps grindstones for sharpening drills were arranged on the level platform to its west.

Smithy and offices of the northern granite quarry (site 23).

A little further downhill is a ruined tiny square building, last used as the manager's toilet but probably first as a magazine for storing the quarry's explosives. Another ruined magazine stands close to the old hollow-way below the main dumps.

24. Major Pasture Boundary

A substantial Cornish hedge (stone faced with earth and stone core), up to 2.5m wide and 1.7m high, divides Kit Hill into two irregular halves. It winds its way up the north-eastern slopes, skirts the summit plateau's southern side, weaves through pits on the west, and then twists away to Kelly Bray. It was built to be stock-proof - a ditch strengthens the uphill side - and it appears to be the remains of an attempt by one or several of Climsland manor's tenants to privatise a portion of Kit Hill's commons. They presumably took the land to the south, more distant but less stony, as the northern block would still have been entered from Downgate, the traditional way onto the summer grazings.

Being so long (over 2 kilometres are contained by the Country Park), the boundary has numerous chronological relationships with other features, riding over or utilising earlier ones (for example lode-back pits and dumps), being cut by or damaged by later ones, and it is possible to use

Later, Non-Industrial

these to calculate a construction date in the last decades of the 18th century.

The considerable effort taken to built this boundary (and others on the north-west and eastern slopes) was apparently wasted as it seems to have been quickly abandoned. There are no signs of routine repairs (blocking of breaches etc) and the boundary was apparently redundant by the early 19th century as it was not recorded on maps of 1813, 1815 or 1840. The benefits the privatisers hoped to gain - separation of healthy, disease-free livestock, the chance to improve the rough grazing, perhaps ultimately the subdivision, enclosure and improvement of their block of moorland clearly did not materialise and Kit Hill reverted to the open commons it had been since prehistoric times. More recently, from the mid 19th century to the first few decades of the 20th, farmers gradually enclosed the Hill's lower slopes with much smaller fields, bounded by ruler-straight but often poorly built walls and hedges. A number of wholly new farms and smallholdings were established, places like Clitters, Claremont and Hingston Farm.

25. Folly

On Kit Hill's summit, immediately south of the car park, is this five-sided enclosure built on a levelled platform and formed by strong earthen banks, the western side largely destroyed. There are circular bastions at four corners, the exception being between the two shorter northern sides where a 3.5m gap was probably the original entrance. The recently partially restored south-west bastion is the best-preserved and the damaged north-east and south-east ones would probably have been identical to it, flat-topped, c 12.5m diameter with vertical stone walling to c 2.5m high. A much grander construction at the north-west node had on top of a steep-sided mound or miniature motte, reaching 3.8m high on its south-west side, a larger circular stone walled chamber or keep, 15.2m diameter. It is now just 0.6m high but was once much higher, having been largely destroyed by later 19th century mining activities, including the building of the mine wind engine and then the great chimney stack which now stands on it.

Sir John Call's folly (site 25) at the summit of the hill, as portrayed on a pound note issued by Kit Hill Bank in the early 19th century (Royal Institution of Cornwall).

There is no external ditch around the enclosure and although its hill-top position is dramatic, it is also militarily vulnerable as the Hill's rounded profile renders all slopes invisible, creating dangerous dead ground. These factors have made the enclosure's interpretation problematic but interesting. It appears to be a defended site, a primitive fort, and was given statutory protection as a Scheduled Monument by archaeologists suggesting it might have been a Civil War (1640s) defended camp, even though there was no documentary evidence to support this. The enclosure was subsequently re-interpreted by an industrial archaeologist as a reservoir storing water for use in the mining complex to the north and during restoration the entrance was given a sluice-like stile (now removed).

Not satisfied with this interpretation, other archaeologists returned to the Civil War earthwork theory only to be thwarted again by the discovery of obscure documents recording the construction in the late 18th century on top of Kit Hill of a mock

Partially reconstructed south-west bastion of Sir John Call's folly (site 25). The chimney stack stands on the motte which originally supported a mock keep.

Saxon castle. This is clearly our site, with the north-west mound a motte and the enclosure a kind of bailey. It did not work defensively because it was just a fancy. Its builder was Sir John Call of Whiteford, near Stoke Climsland, the local squire and MP, and a veteran of military campaigns in India. He intended his castle to be a monument to the battle of Hingston Down of 838 when the Anglo-Saxon King Egbert's routing of a mixed Cornish-Danish army, probably actually towards the Gunnislake end of Hingston Down, saw Cornwall's resistance finally subdued. The enclosure is, then, an important archaeological site, a memorial to Cornish nationalism, and an unusual folly.

26. Circular Enclosures

Fairly evenly spaced, 85 and 105m apart, on the higher western and north-western slopes are three enigmatic circular enclosures. They are all about 30m diameter internally and were apparently built in the 17th or 18th centuries, most likely the latter judging from the fairly fresh appearance of their steeply sloping earth

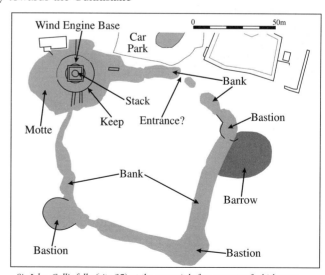

Sir John Call's folly (site 25) at the summit before recent refurbishment.

The Archaeology of Kit Hill   **47**

and stone banks, up to 2.4m wide and 1.6m high externally, and their external ditches, up to 0.7m deep. The northern enclosure has been almost entirely devoured by the main granite quarry - only its southern edge survives although it was shown complete on 19th century OS maps.

Interpretation of these sites is uncertain. They are unlikely to be pens, or pounds, as the external ditches were designed to keep stock out, not in. Other possibilities, such as fodder stores or preaching places, founder when consideration is taken of their uniqueness of design (found only on Kit Hill), their multiplicity (why three?), their exposed locations (the windiest quarter), their even spacing neither particularly close together nor far apart, their apparent lack of original entrances (livestock have since forced a number of breaches through the banks).

The circles remain a puzzle and the CAU and the Estates Officer would welcome any suggestions as to their purpose. A current favourite is that the folly builder Sir John Call threw them up to supplement his summit castle (site 25), perhaps as representations of enemy camps or siegeworks. We might imagine them being used in strange romantic entertainments, re-enactments of the Battle of Hingston Down. Revellers could picnic within them and look away down onto Call's Whiteford mansion.

27. Boundstones

No less than 18 boundstones have been recorded within the Country Park although they are rarely seen, being mainly either along its edges or in the heavily overgrown north-west sector.

The most attractive stones are the beautifully dressed granite pillars, up to 1.75m high, with pyramidal tops, set up in 1845 by the Duchy of Cornwall to mark the southern boundary of Stoke Climsland manor's wastes. There had been legal disputes concerning this and other moorland Duchy manors' wastes (Rillaton Manor, for example, has similar stones near Minions). Three, numbered 6 to 8, are within the Country Park, all with SC 1845 carefully inscribed on their northern faces.

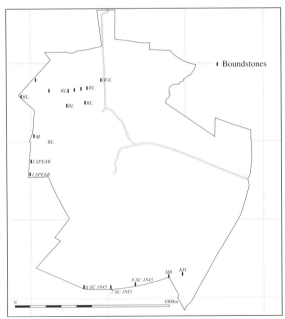

Boundstones on Kit Hill. Not all carry inscriptions.

48   The Archaeology of Kit Hill

A little earlier and just as interesting are the eight stones set up in 1815 to define sides of a block of land on the north-west slopes called Robinsland - six of the roughly split stones have RL cut into them. The Duchy had again been involved in a legal dispute, this time with its own tenants, regarding the taking of stone from these slopes. They commissioned a survey to establish the bounds and had the stones erected. Robinsland itself has medieval origins as 'Rubandesland', an area of rough grazing from which certain Stoke Climsland tenants could remove building stone. Being such poor land and an island within a sea of commons, it appears to have never been given physical bounds (hedge, ditch or stones) until these early 19th century tenants attempted to establish a commercial quarrying enterprise, against the Duchy's own interests. Most of the Robinsland stones are now inaccessible but one stands in the north-west corner of the Country Park beside the bridle-way entrance from Kelly Bray and another alongside the horse trail.

Early 19th century Robinsland (RL) boundstone (site 27).

On the Hill's south-east slopes are two small boundstones, one with KH on its north face, the other with HB on its west face. The former has its inscription looking up to the Kit Hill mining sett whose bounds were mapped passing through this point in 1848. The HB stone may also refer to a mine sett, perhaps an extension of the famous Holmbush mine to the north-west - the inscription is unlikely to relate to Harrowbarrow (in Calstock parish) as it faces the wrong way. The possibility remains, however, that the initials are those of an individual. Three other stones bear the names or initials of the tenants who enclosed parts of the lower western slopes; two with I.SPEAR, one with M.

In keeping with these old boundstones, the waymarked trail uses granite inscribed with a representation of the summit stack.

Further Reading

This booklet is based on:

Herring, P C and Thomas, S N H, *The Archaeology of Kit Hill*, 2nd edition, 1990, also available from CAU for £10.

With the exception of Ann Eade's delightful booklet (see below) there is very little other literature directly concerned with Kit Hill. The following will help you pursue particular themes:

Barnatt, J, *Prehistoric Cornwall, The Ceremonial Monuments*, Turnstone Press, 1982

Barton, D B, *The Mines and Mineral Railways of East Cornwall and West Devon*, Bradford Barton, 1964

Bishop, G, *A Parish Album of Stoke Climsland*, Columbian, 1987

Booker, F, *The Industrial Archaeology of the Tamar Valley*, David and Charles, 1967

Cornwall Archaeological Unit, *Cornwall's Archaeological Heritage*, Twelveheads Press, 1990

Eade, A, *Kit Hill, Our Hill*, Columbian, 1989

Eade, A, *Kit Hill Aureole*, Columbian, 1993

Earl, B, *Cornish Mining*, Bradford Barton, 1968

Jenkin, A K H, *Mines and Miners of Cornwall*, Vol 15, Calstock, Callington and Launceston, Forge Books, 1969

Lightbody, S R, *The Book of Callington*, Barracuda, 1982

Stanier, P, *Quarries and Quarrying*, Shire, 1985

Acknowledgements

Special thanks to Nigel Thomas of CAU who assisted in the original survey of Kit Hill, helped write the main report and made useful comments on this booklet. Cathy Parkes, Steve Scoffin, Richard Walton, Colin Buck, Caroline Vulliamy, Mary Atkinson, Nicholas Johnson, Peter Rose, Adam Sharpe, Jacky Nowakowski and Mike Hawkey also made valuable comments.

Liskeard Rd. Callington. Tel. Liskeard 383215

The Chantry Guest House is a family run business. Colour T.V. in bedrooms, H+C, Tea & Coffee facilities.

Open all year round.

Three Cottages on a working farm in the tranquil Tamar Valley. Ideally situated to explore the Industrial Heritage and walking the Tamar Trail.

Self Catering Cottages

English Tourist Board Graded

Contact B.J. Howlett
Deer Park Farm, Luckett, Callington. PL17 8NW
Fax or Phone 01579 370292

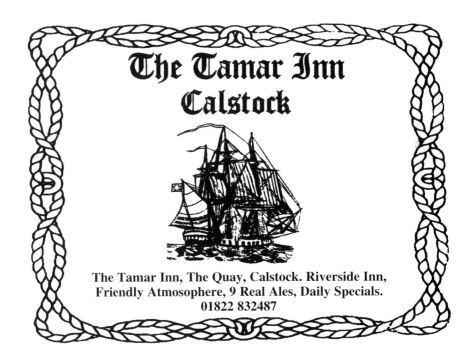

The Tamar Inn
Calstock

The Tamar Inn, The Quay, Calstock. Riverside Inn,
Friendly Atmosphere, 9 Real Ales, Daily Specials.
01822 832487

Cadson Manor Farm

Callington, Cornwall, PL17 7HW

Tel/Fax: (01579) 383969

Approx. 4 miles from KIT HILL, on the A390 Callington to Liskeard route. Adjacent to historic Cadson Bury. Two acre lake stocked with coarse fish. Farm and Lynher River walks.

4 keys Highly Commended self catering accommodation in wing of manor house sleeps up to 6. Extensive views of fishing lake and Cadson Bury. B&B also available, en suite. Brochure available.

Cadson Farm's impressive entrance incorporates two large granite pillars which probably came from Kit Hill. Over the centuries people have carved their names in these entrance stones, the earliest date we have found is 16th century. At Newbridge, below the farm, the A390 crosses the Lynher River by a 15th Century bridge. Within living memory an extra horse would have been hired at the Toll House (now a private house) by the bridge to assist in the haul up to the "take off" stone located by the entrance to Cadson Manor. Nowadays our visitors arrive by modern transport but can enjoy the past around them while staying in a level of comfort their predecessors could not possibly have imagined.

The Morwellham and Tamar Valley Trust

Morwellham Quay, Nr. Tavistock, Devon PL19 8JL

Visitor Centre and open-air Museum, established in 1970 to preserve, display and interpret the history and geography of Morwellham, Tamar River Port.

Visitors can ride by electric train tramway (3.5 ton BEV battery electric locomotion) underground into the George and Charlotte copper mine, last worked in 1869. Visible copper ore seams. Displays of mining techniques. Working 5.5m diameter underground waterwheel.

A wooden ship - Merchant Sailing ketch 'Garlandstone' launched from Calstock in 1908, is under restoration in Devon Consuls Dock, and can usually be boarded.

Shire horses pull wagonettes for visitor rides along part of the Duke of Bedford's old carriageway.

A section of the Tavistock Canal towpath can be viewed. Docks. Quays. Ore-chutes. Early rail track remains. Inclined planes. Water-wheel. Leats. Lime-kilns. Workshops. Cottages. Stables. Water powered threshing machine.

Staff wear reproduction costume and visitors can try on costumes themselves.

Marsh and woodland nature reserve on the Devon Bank of the River Tamar. Waymarked trails and observation hides.

Museums, Video shows, Demonstrations and activities, some especially for children.

Open all year (except Christmas) 10.00 am - 5.30 pm daily, reduced operation in winter with early closing.

Family tickets, concessions and group rates.

Located - 4 miles from Tavistock off A390.
Map reference - SX 446 697

Rail/bus - Tamar Valley Line/Western National.

Morwellham and Tamar Valley Trust. (reg.charity No. 261361) Nr. Tavistock, West Devon. PL 19 8JL.

Tel. 01822 832766 (833808 fax and recorded information)

The Archaeology of Kit Hill **53**

The National Trust
COTEHELE
St. Dominick, Saltash, Cornwall, PL12 6TA

Cotehele was owned by the Edgcumbe family for nearly 600 years and passed to the National Trust in 1947. It is now managed and protected by the National Trust for the benefit of visitors with a wide range of tastes and interests.

This fascinating and enchanting estate on the steep wooded slopes above the River Tamar, offers....

* One of the least altered medieval houses in the country, containing a fine collection of furniture, textiles and tapestries.

* Formal gardens and a richly planted valley garden.

* Cotehele Quay, a busy port in Victorian times, with an art and craft gallery, maritime museum, ice cream sales and licensed tea room.

* An old estate corn mill restored to working order with a range of agricultural buildings with collections of tools nearby.

* Woodland and riverside walks.

* A 15th Century barn with licensed restaurant, shop and plant sales.

Open April - October
House and Mill closed Fridays
but Mill open Fridays in July and August.
Garden and estate walks all year.

EVENTS & ENQUIRIES
Please phone (01579) 351346

Callington Museum Liskeard Road, Callington

Open April - October, Friday, Saturday, Sunday and Bank Holidays 10 - 4pm. We are happy to open at any other time by arrangement. School parties welcome.

Permanent display of local prehistory, mining and models of Callington c1840 and Callington Station. Also three different exhibitions each season.

We hold nearly 7000 items - including local artefacts, minerals, books, documents, maps, plans, memorabilia, posters, postcards and photographs.

If you are interested in the history of South East Cornwall through the ages we have something to offer you.

For further details contacts Julie Johns on 01822 832898

Polhilsa Farm

Callington, Cornwall   Tel 01579 370784

Open all year (except Christmas)

Lakeside accommodation in 300 year old farm house. Spacious comfortable rooms with guests own bathroom. TV lounge. Ideal for touring north and south coast, moors & National Trust properties. Leisure facilities and good eating houses within easy reach.

Over Tamar Bridge to roundabout. Take 3rd exit to Callington. Remaining on A388 through Callington and Kelly Bray. Left at next crossroads (signposted Golberdon). Take first right leading to farm.

Trehorner Farm Holiday Park

Lower Metherell, Callington, PL17 8BJ
Tel: (01579) 3551122

Open April to October

Located in the beautiful Tamar Valley, Trehorner Farm offers peace and tranquillity for a relaxed holiday in our luxury 'Rose Award' holiday homes. Our facilities include a children's playground, secluded heated swimming pool, mini golf, sauna and solarium. Young children have fun feeding the ducks, geese and sheep, not forgetting 'Freeway' the goat and 'Becky' the Shetland pony.
Nearby is the 15th century inn.